LEYLINES OF MY FLESH

LEYLINES OF MY FLESH

Vivian Hansen

Touchwood Press

National Library of Canada Cataloguing in Publication Data

Hansen, Vivian, 1957-
 Leylines of My Flesh

 Poems.
 Includes index.
 ISBN 0-9687861-2-X

 1. Immigrants--Canada--Poetry. 2. Danes--Canada--Poetry. I. Title.
PS8565.A5893L49 2002   C811'.54   C2002-910821-7
PR9199.3.H36L49 2002

Touchwood Press
6228 Touchwood Drive NW
Calgary AB T2K 3L9
E-mail: touchwoodpress@msn.com

Editing for the Press: Cecelia Frey
Guest Editor: Catherine Fuller
Book Design & Production: John Frey
Cover Design: Noelle Der
Visuals from weavings on Dutch plankloom: Liv Pedersen
    Cover title: "Tail Gating"

Printed and bound in Canada by Priority Printing Limited of Edmonton, Alberta

to my father and mother, Eduard Hansen
and Anna Kjestine Petersen, and

to my daughter Alexis Joy Hansen Winning

TABLE OF CONTENTS

GLOSSARY

BEDSTEFAR: grandfather
BEDSTEMOR: grandmother
DALE: to fall; the essence of inanimate objects, such
      as trees or leaves, as they fall
DÍSIR: the divine grandmothers, a collective of female
      deities concerned with fertility. At the moment of birth,
      the dísir took action on behalf of mother and child.
FAR: father
FAR MOR: father's mother
FUGL: bird
HÅNDARBEJDE: needlework; the prayer of hands
JORDMOR: earth mother; midwife
KÆRLIGHED: the state of being in love
MOSTER: mother's sister
NORNS: in Norse mythology, the Fates, three wise women
      spinners who determined a life span. They were aged
      hags or crones, respected by all for their immense
      power. It is said that even Odin was subject to their
      power.
OLDEMOR: great-grandmother
OLDEFAR: great-grandfather
RUNESTENEN: rune stones, or the grave markers of
      Vikings
SKYLD: the norn who governs the future
URD (WYRD/WEIRD): the norn who governs the past
VERDANDI: the norn who governs the present
YGGDRASIL: the Norse World Tree, which connected all
      the worlds and held the universe together. The three
      norns were responsible for watering the tree, thus
      preserving the fabric of all creation.

Leylines: the straight tracks of our ancestors that mark our position and direction via landmarks such as earth mounds, forest paths, clumps of trees and runestenen.

HÅNDARBEJDE

Handiwork: The Prayer of Hands

The Clothesline

HÅNDARBEJDE

(for Liv)

she pulls at meditation
fine wools that weave faces,
cars, skipping ropes,
laughing children at play
animation
invited into her studio.

træd min gæst
i stuen ind
her er ly for
regn og vind

she weaves tactile wool
into place, into covenant
with memory and the present tense
of onions, remoulade, roast beef and shrimp,
a luncheon spread
for my questions
my theories about woman-strength.

the soft woollen knowing
behind Danish words, beckoning
welcome, forming a tapestry of fingers,
showing how a woman, Viking, warrior
reproduces reflection
in a slow weave

meditating.

TWISTING AND TWINING

Bedstemor likes crocheting
building tapestries, weaving destinations
of her life arbejde, into fate knots.
I have her needlepoint pillowcover
her stitches of deer suspended
leaping over bloodied poppies
and grey, embossed partridges sitting
in perpetual, unnatural, green trees.

Bedstemor refuses
to name the tree Yggdrasil
denies knowing the place of its roots
near Asgård, where the gods met.

Bedstemor would never
speak about Wyrd's well
where she seeks water
where the gods once held
daily assembly.

Bedstemor performs
håndarbejde, twisting threads
like a new Norn biding a new time
in which she may not speak
of what women know.
håndarbejde is life-arbejde.

she will not name herself as Wyrd
weaver of fate
keeper of the well where the gods once met
beneath an unnaturally green
Yggdrasil.

NAMING AN ANCESTOR

I sense her in that ineffable *something*
where all suggestions count
becoming the true transcendence
of life and art
like the maple tree rising
taller than windows
built to look at it.

she whose story is lost
except for her baptism
and confirmation
and the fist she slammed on the Danish Folketing
the census in 1745
giving her full name
Anna-Christina Nicolajsdatter
Nicolaj's Daughter.

she who knew *something* of love and eternity
enough to ride them as waves unwounded by rocks,
slipping, dying, into tide pools
where I can still pick the shells of her vulva.

ANCESTRAL ROSES

Her er en Rose lagt Trotz Edens Rosmariner
Christi Roser af de rareste Christiner
(here lies a rose fairer than Eden's rose garden
of Christ's Roses, the rarest Christina)
    H.A. Brorson, at Christina Brorson's funeral, 19 June 1721

western Canada, December 31 1999
about 4:00 pm
I wait for graves to open
in rural Denmark

the blessed dead rising
singing hymns of roses
and winging upwards to Heaven
in millennial draft.

I see living souls flutter
scatter like petals from a great rose
in a grey Bedsted churchyard
where the Danes say Brorson planted a rose bush
in honour of his secret love,
his brother's wife.

he took a cutting of a woman
grafted her into my flesh,
clean. wet. fecund.
I felt
a tremor
my flesh shifting shape
to ancestral stones

my bones
singing
the cadence of roses.

MINNA/LOUISA

twins separated
by ocean and prairie leys.

when Tante Minna sews seeds
pansy faces and dragon snaps
into the seams of my skirts
she has known for a long time
she will not return to Denmark.

she knows
that the pail of gooseberries
Louisa promised her
will never be filled.

I watch her pluck these furry *stikklesbær*
from a bush in Canada
memory stalling her pluck.
her blue eyes saddening, becoming berries
rounding at the memory of her twin sister
and at the back of her eyes
a bedstemor long dead.

the bulge of berries
cloning, twinning
        over a tin pail.

POESI 1

(for Anna-Lise)

```
        L
V       E       L
        V
```

Glem dig ej din vugge
og ej din Moders Lykke
vokser du fra barnekaar
Glem dig ej dit 'Fader vor'
Glem dig ej din Vugge
        til minde om
        Ragnhild Haugaard
        Bedsted, January 28, 1945

LIVE WELL
forget not your cradle
and your mother's arms
as you grow up

I've gazed so long
at blossoms and boundaries
of shiny paper roses
in your autograph book.
I try to paste glossy roses
around your face, Tante Anna-Lise,
think you into a girl
as you give me your book of autographs
childish poems.

our faces as similar
as old and new moons.
we dream the same sweet reds of roses
in hues of moonlight.

forget not your 'our father'
forget not your cradle

remembering
the anaphora of Danish, sounding
like the clack of your dirty shoes
against pine railroad ties
in old Calgary
travelled
years and ties and worries later
away
from your mother's arms.

POESI 2

(for Anna-Lise)

Fuglen synger fra sin Rolig
den er glad i ringe kaar
bliv som den, til freds og roglig
glæd dig I din Ungdoms aar
    til minde om
    Søren Peter Hansen
    Bedsted, February 5, 1945

your friend does not name the fugl
whose voice you hear
dimly
from the short springtime
in Calgary.

Søren's best advice
to be like the bird
satisfied, and still
happy in your youth

is a cadence far from chickadee
or toppling baby robins
assertive jays wrestling for seed
the birds you tend in your own forest.

a new poem
wrought from birds
in your old age, words as harsh and plaintive
as a killdeer on prairie.

IMPEDIMENTA

(for Rit Svane Wengel 1887-1959)

*Far from here in a strange country there is a rock one mile long, one mile
wide, one mile high. Every hundred years a small bird will come to that
rock and sharpen its beak on the rock. When in this way the rock is worn
out, the first second of eternity has passed.*

(Old Danish proverb)

i

a lexicon for pain
ache. her work.
the tiresome, endless, detestable struggle
against dirt and struggle matters
so little.
her work
beside a man, the effort
so completely useless
hurts
far more than a broken arm
a sore side
an empty purse.

Rit re-members
her oldemor's white-scrubbed floors
etched with straw-balls of sand.
she picks from the stain of prairie
grass balls wet of rain, to scrub.

one octave lower than memory
is Paul, mere man, her husband
who seeps uncertainly into merging geology
the strata of Canada.

forever sure of a peasant's life in Denmark
his manhood now confused
beside the perennial pink flower of Rit
blooming between fieldstones.

ii

we have to depend on man's memory
Harald Bluetooth, buried next to *Runestenen*
in Roskilde, a stone's throw from Rit's birthplace
she grows into the knowing of what men can do
in the service of kings, her sea-captain father
forming a layer of sea-strata
foaming, hardening
resolve.
Rit does not apprehend
weeds.
beaten: not of economical conditions,
want, work or
loneliness;
I could gladly fight that
till my last day – but of a man's indifference.

iii

I shall keep his clothes and
make the meals but
don't ask me
to bring along anything
so unwanted as love.
it is far too chilly, where Paul is around,
for such a fair thing to live and thrive.

iv

pink, sacred paint, peeled from weathered
boards, time's fuschia faded
a falsehood of crimson, a delicacy
of memory.
Rit is surprised
at the blessing of colour.
the sun is setting in clouds of
rose, amber, blue and violet.

I lean my arms upon the windowsill
and gaze
on nature's glory and pray that not all,
all my dreams of past will vanish
like the glowing mist not leaving
the slightest trace
of all love and hope.

she is patching a life
the håndarbejde of hope
consoles herself
the homestead cannot be sold
without
my
consent.

she refuses the turkey plucking job
lives in a houseful of dead mice
where twenty years of dust storms gather behind paper.
turns herself
into a bird.

v

peace that passes all understanding occurs
in a Danish beechwood in spring
a crocus in the Sandhills across the Saskatchewan River,
the somber voice of the wind in a spruce forest.
Rit can fly, now.
the home farm cannot be sold without my
consent.

Rit inhales holiness
where light and shadows play
in canyons or between
majestic trees; a great peace
is in my soul, more than
any word from any man could ever bring.

she travels an old Indian trail
follows the creek into mystery miles
and miles and miles
into the mountains
that lift their white heads into the clouds, the creek cuts
its way through the moss and fernclad sides
ceaseless.

vi

I lean my arms upon the windowsills
watch a sunset.
it seems to strike all the drifting clouds
and fogbanks from underneath
so the mountains are floating steel blue
violet, white and black
in amber and rose seas.

The homestead cannot be sold without my consent.

Rit leans her dreams on her windowsill
to look at peace
listening, seeing
the colour of the sill is pink
                pink
                   pink.

SKOAL

(for Inge)

Skoal: a toast that comes from the ancient Viking tradition of severing the head of an enemy, rendering it, removing the brains, and drinking ale from the skull.

Skoal!
she shares
her knowing of animals
of cows alive, pregnant
with the sliding caress of a woman.

the vet is impressed
how well a Danish woman knows
her livestock.

she knows
because her father turned fear-white
when their sow died after birthing twelve piglets
the whole family, including little girls,
slept in the hay, arms extending bottles of milk
feeding our own food.

such stories dissolve Inge's eyes into tears.

she knows what to do with cows
knows how to feed them
knows how to sleep with them
when her man leaves.
he has never understood
the tenderness of her knowing.
dumber than a cow
he does not discern
that she is gentle with him,

that she knows how to love a man
who knows how to feed his woman.

she asks me
*do you know what the Viking women did
when their men mistreated them?*

they cut off their heads!

she clinks her ale glass against mine,
cheeks rosy
voice thirsty
she shouts
Skoal!

SPEAKING TO NORNS

I challenged the Norns to tell me
about themselves
my thoughts ready
waiting to write.

Verdandi stepped out of the present
in a fit of righteous pique
and broke my writing arm.
muttering something about
listening to the quiet fugue
in the points of a winter sunbeam
or gazing
at stars that needle the black sky.

then, what I thought I knew
Wyrd laughed at, she who is also called
Urd, the Norse knower of word
and all things spoken by my ancestors.

when I looked into the future
and asked Skyld
what my name would be
she calls me broken-wing
a poet

or, she who visits with Norns
and learns to listen
with her bones.

SCRIBE

I imagine myself
five years old
colouring on walls.
I put
round flowers just there
in a wheel of colour.

I put
protolanguage on walls
reds and greens and blues
crayon wax forests
fireworks perpetually
suspended.

she who is lodged in my throat
is a curious crimson poppy.

I lift her on a stool, a pedestal
and give her the wall
so she can transfer
sound into colour.

she insists on bruised purple bananas
yellow grapes
orange apples
venturing outside the lines
just because they are black and presume to be
impenetrable.
what is *wrong* is scripted
in these black shades
of demarcation.

what is heard
is on the other side of the wall
a child's knock.
her mother apologizes for all the noise.

I wonder if I colour with
indigo blue
ruby red
magenta
suspended
if the colour will penetrate
the firewall.

STRAINER

knowing how
needing the right equipment
unnamed
kitchen
utensils.

knowing its shape and feel
the potato-sigh of steam rising
keeping heat from my fingers.

this thing
necessary to cooking
I grope my mind's lexicon
touch my tongue to sounds
sibilants, short
like boiling water rushing through
prepared holes.

my husband says
you need the colander.
colander
a complicated pattern of English sounds
I strain to my mother's word
I need a *si.*
si   si

JORDMOR

Earth Mother: Midwife

Self-Portrait '88

EARTH MOTHER

she tells me she was jordmor
to lots of babies in Denmark
and hoped for the same courtesy
birthing me here.

but Canadians disapproved
of Danish women who knew about fertility.
her goddesses of dísir summoned to aid her birth, silenced
in soughing, June, prairie winds.

the doctor and nurses strapped her to a gurney,
afraid of her foreign words.
they said it was the only way
they could subdue her power
as she birthed me into screaming Danish, calling
on the dísir to make way, help her birth
a breech baby girl.

Junes later, she readies the earth for pansies
and digs too deep.
she clumps the soil into my small hand.
we've dug down to min syvendedel Oldemor.

I examine the black pungent spring soil
looking for pieces
of my mother's seventh great-grandmother
while Mom laughs at her own power.

DANCE ON ROSES

roses proliferate
in Denmark,
red petals
like the memory of lips

an offering to the dead.
dried kisses intended
for eternity
babies buried thus
smothered in roses.

when I hear the cliché
that Far Mor's life
was no *dans på roser*,
I press all the uses for roses
into sounds.

I imagine Far Mor
screaming a baby girl into death
before birth
small parts dismembered
by a drunken country doctor

stillborn 1924
this remainder of a baby's name
no more than parts and petals from a withered rose
pressed between the pages
of Far Mor's old Bible.

MOTHER, IN FRAGMENTS

i

you spoke of your baby's death
as you might describe
a needlepoint picture
each thread sewn diligently
to make a whole, small, tapestry.

the roses that lay beside her
fresh, red
her finger touching petals
stripped from thorns
you took no chance she might
prick herself
strangle the horror of whooping cough
into the sounds of eternity.

ii

you spoke of Lone's death
at last you minted the words
to speak the sight of her in a small coffin
pressed their weight upon your own eyes
to gage
the plenitude of their sound.

ROAD OF GENERATIONS

cobbled from old seas and salt
immeasurable.
my bedstefar and I
amble between ancient longhouses
Viking hearths, thatch
that cloaks the roof of Oldefar's house.

this road is full of ancestors: Bedstefar, Oldefar,
shadowed with memories
of strolling geese
pigs
milk cows
dray horses working the fields.

along the godly roundness of stones
I sweat breast milk
suppress English while I speak to Bedstefar, stroll with him
along old paths he wants me to see right now
while I try to dream peace into this time of being
a new mother.

beyond the wet chasm of an ocean that steals my self
and cleaves me from ancestral men.
he murmurs to me in a language
I cannot name.
we are connecting
by umbilical speech,
a strange patriarchy of Viking peasants,
kin.

I press my baby's skin to my own
where she drinks in Danish words, suckles
from my dream of Bedstefar.
moves her mouth
over cobblestones.

TEA LEAVES AND LOVE

kærlighed, state of being
pressed into liquid motion.

we say I love you
like tea dripping through a strainer
into what we swallow.
elskov, beloved
a verb tensed to taste
all essence.

the meanings of love caught.
like leaves in tea
distilling.

EXHAUST OF MEMORY

red streaks in the sky
remind me of my bedstefar.

ice dust and particles
of atmosphere
carbon, leftover fossils,
cells of skin and Viking bones
exhaust of fossils.

the reminder, pictures from Denmark
where every sunset is streaked with blazing light
and Bedstefar's sepia bones, like fossils
guard the other, old, world.

FUGL'S CHOICE

I give her a human shape.
she trips, steps on stilted bird legs
feigns a broken wing.
choosing to be
prey
assuming
female-ness, protecting her eggs
preferring the nesting ground
     of farm fields
     lawns
     airfields.

she nests in a campground
seems eager for weekend punishment
from city folk, dogs, wild children
her wing perpetually
slumped
in an act of love.

she is killdeer
prairie mother.
I cannot watch the limits of her sacrifice.
she refuses to extend her wings.
if she were to fly
instead of protecting her eggs
there would be nothing to comprehend
nothing I could apprehend
of mothering, of *morskab.*

FOLLOW YOUR HEART

around its curves
predictable like the 14th of February
pink like Far Mor's fingers
and the upside-down curve of her bum
or the same symmetry
of her breasts.

following her woman's heart at the curve of the millennium
meant believing in stone circles of choice
or believing in the choice of choice or
that her heart had a pointer,
a divining rod that would make
a decision
when it bent before an underground spring
incognita.

following her heart was a portion of illusion
eighty years ago, when she was housekeeper for a man
who was good to her
and sought to satisfy her need
before his own.

and so, when her belly grew great with child
and nestled under her breast
she knew
there was no such thing as choice.

ELSKOV

I am my beloved's
and his desire is for me
Come, my beloved, let us go out into the country
Let us spend the night in the village.

(Song of Solomon 7: 10-11)

the word
conjures an earthy forest in Bedsted
where trees were taller
in the Danish part of my childhood.

back then
there were elves
who needed rice pudding to pacify their prancing
beneath Danish ferns, in a dark forest
I danced with them, a stone's throw

from my bedstefar's grave in the village
where he slept
close to a skipping granddaughter he never knew.

I hear whispers of *elskov*
beloved
a liquid sound in either language
meaning something treasured
in a forest
full of elves dancing in circles
beneath beech trees.

elskov is a wish
      your breath exhales in wonder
      as you touch a breast with your Danish tongue.

CONVEX BABY

when I make my announcement
my Jewish friend speaks *L'Chaim.*

as I lie still in bed on a January morning
my baby somersaults her first flutters
becoming.

my belly rises above the waters of my bath
convex
like a glacial drumlin
the dance of life much faster now.

mmmmmm   unspeakable
moan of my baby's primal words sound
her displeasure aimed at me
low, tired, angry
so different from the dadadadad
she taps in lucky-baby code to her dad
when she is content.

these images have no words
utterance refusing articulation
in the time lapse of her bloom
sixteen now, she suspends
my poetry
with her talk.

my smile at her is the sign that
my nipples woke me this morning
tugged by tenacity of memory
that utters no word.
only gusto
and pleasure.

LILIES

a thirsty summer coolness lingers
in my mother's garden
a clubhouse for lilies.

I pluck their black seed coins
until Mom shouts
you'll steal their babies!

they stick their tiny fingers
into fuzzy stamen finger puppets
green throats form petals of Eros
drinking my mother's secrets.

lilies wait.
arms folded behind their backs
casually.
stamens fingering air
losing dew, luring
the sun.

they form secret reading societies
where they thrum soft cayenne notes
to each other.

THATCH

the longhouse wears thatch
like an old woollen coat
drooping comfortably over door frames,
impervious to rain.
thatch covers the birthing place
of all my mother's stories.

Bedstemor catches her foretelling
the neighbour will die.
my four-year-old mother cannot explain
how she knows
but sees it in his gait, hears it in his cough,
raw thatch drying
over his head.
he is dead in a week.

Bedstefar says
>   *my little girl*
>   *when you know these things*
>   *you must never say them out loud,*
>   *except to me. I will protect you.*

when lightning strikes
a neighbour's thatched roof
she watches
a little girl praying to the God
her Far believes in.

as she and Bedstefar gape in terror
the flames leap over his longhouse
catch another neighbour's roof.
roaring
to the conducting tenor
of my mother's prayers.

the longhouses either side
blaze to blackened ground.
her home sits safe
untouched, green
cloaked in cool thatch.

when she finds her tongue
she tells only Bedstefar
what she has done.

IMMIGRATION

Vi skulle aldrig ses igen
...we should never see each other again

en lille ting at mindes dem ved
…a little thing to remember them by

They are things. just things, mother.
I want your breath
your stories whispered to me
the tales unplated with silver's unnatural sheen
the stories I live in the leylines of my flesh.

I am reading this story of yours
the safe one you write for thousands of eyes
that will read
and weep for your fate.

immigration
or *springing over the Atlantic*
doused
in an ocean of tears.

forty years of English has dried those fonts
so well, you dare not recall the anguish
as you speak of your journey across Canada.

you speak instead of the pieces of silver gleaned
from your bedstemor
before you left Denmark, weeping
for losses
you refuse to speak into being
your new tongue caught
between the barbs of two languages.

DALE

The life essence of leaves or snowflakes, as they fall

Bicycling

UDVANDRER

what possesses a man
to leave his fatherland?
his safe job as postman? his pension?
the newspaper reporter
aghast at my father's choices.

my mother is silent, posing for the camera
my brother Thorkild
is the only one smiling
unaware
that my father spoke to the headmaster
last week, and learned
that a postman's son
no matter how clever
will never matriculate
will never go to university.

what the black and white news
will not print
is that my father would rather
begin again with his woman, his sons.

my father
would rather
harvest crops he does not know,
change his title to landmand, farmer.
he would rather sacrifice his pension
than feed his son
to a Danish class system.

he has only just told my mother:
we are *all* leaving.

SENSE OF ROADS

the leylines across an ocean
expanse of prairie
settle in my mother's sense of roads.
she is used to shorter navigations
no detours
Jersey milk cows
in wet, peat pastures.

I wonder if the dimensions of immigration are too big for us?
she writes, expansively
locating dimension.
her intuitions reformatted
in geometric terms.

the switch
seems necessary
to apprehend a prairie landscape
flexed, grainy muscle
beyond
the practical joke
of a mere detour.

the prairie is ribboned
in barbed wire.

FIRST WORDS

Uncle Hans' homestead
is called *a place.*

as Uncle Arnold drives south from Edmonton
he tries to explain
how *a place* is like a Danish *gaard.*
the Danes understand
although the Engelsk do not,
the meaning of the names
Præstegaard, Kirkegaard.
these are the *places*
where the priest lives
where the church resides.

a *place*
is a house
or a tipi near Hobbema
the *place* where Indians live.

this *place* interests my brother
who wants to see a real tipi
a central hearth smoking through a tent of skins, or canvas
like a wood stove in a Viking longhouse.

a place is a house, or tipi.

my parents and my brothers
learn their first words in English
secondary only to
a stick of chewing gum.

in
visible colour

Nearly all authorities on Canadian Immigration concur in the opinion that the very best immigrants that have come to Canada from foreign countries are those from Iceland, Sweden, Norway and Denmark, and it is a very gratifying feature of the tide finding its way to our shores that it still contains a substantial portion of these peoples, whilst a handsome contribution of this fine stock is annually donated by the United States.

Wetaskiwin Times
July 28, 1921

of Vikings.
every painter knows
a primer permits
colour to adhere
to surface.

a survey of names
Jensen, Petersen, Christensen, Krogh,
tight like brussel sprouts
green balls that stick to spine
improving in frost
lending the taste of ground
to stock.

my folk
are big.
taller than the beams of longhouses
built for my ancestors.
longer than an ocean.
my brother should have rowed Viking ships.
my mother bore him so easily
never dreaming
his self would be stock
in visible
to Canada.

A SQUARE MILE

bedroom language
fills with anguished passion
the syntax of my mother's defeat.
her eyes become dry sandstone rocks
eroded, sticking out of the ribs of coulees.

she cannot perceive colour, here
or see
that orange
is the spit of divine sighs soughing
through barley, bowing to air.

I want to tell her about this colour.
I wait to slip into the homestead
like an errant seed
that those with breath, whipped by their own winds
cannot see from where it comes
or where it goes.

I move, unnoticed
into the lexicon of their flesh
as they
exhale.

in October
my mother learns she is pregnant
my father has finished the harvest.

she loses sense, like a precious stone dropped
unaware. her flesh runs in the field
a damaged doe bloodied and terrified
with the barbed wire, a square mile measured
in her flight to nothing. nowhere.

her body stops.
she wakes to her own voice
screaming
higher than the syntax of wind.

FOUNDATIONS

St. Paul Minnesota, February 27, 1959

no one speaks of the rift
between Thor and my father.
the one that measures the size of their horns.

they would rather speak of Thor's
intelligence, his opportunity to become
a Lutheran minister in Minnesota.

Thor writes
when the foundation to the church is built.
the cornerstone, a piece of concrete he can use to scratch
the velvet of his new horns
bloodied and sunbaked.

the pastor's wife faints
from a cut to her finger, delaying
a church service.
no one speaks the truth of blood
from a woman's sacrament.

in Lent
what Thor has given up
he never writes about.

FOLDING

a letter folded
like a recipe, into cake batter.
I wondered what folding meant,
to fold into a mixture, conform
to an envelope.

living stiffly at Christmas
my brother misses us all
does not recognize *Jul* in Minnesota.

he writes that he sings
in the *quire*.
does not know himself, signs *Glædelig Jul*
from a lonely boy who wishes he was home,
        your son.
folded fragments of pain.
enveloped
a single corner peels back, speaking
does Dad have enough work, and is he still
        sleeping on the sofa?

REMORSE

St. Paul Minnesota, 27 December 1959

a hint
he shares, hoping Dad's business will grow
to make room for him.

Thor sends me a doll *til Jul*, for Christmas
a no-named doll.
he sends Mom and Dad a camera
tells them to take lots of pictures.

explains that he is too busy to write to Bedstefar *og* Bedstemor
that he is busy and they ought to accept him for who he is
a lazy writer?

Bedstemor says there is not enough of Jesus
in Minnesota.
probably none in Calgary.
and if Thor forgets his Danish
she worries that Jesus must make a new approach
through savage lands.

she aches for him
but cannot see
how his anger has cloaked him
and camouflaged Jesus
in the ways that Thor wears
his new skin.

CIRCULAR FEET

St. Paul Minnesota 29 January 1960

Thor announces
he wants to become a US citizen.
these plans become real
after the dentist drains the abscess from his teeth
the bad teeth he was born with.

Thor says he does not suffer much
watches basketball games
prefers Dana College
to Camrose Lutheran.

he draws a picture of a little girl with curly hair
and circular feet, pushing a doll carriage.
how he presses his tongue to bad teeth
does not matter.

he knows I can read
his pictures.

WATERMARK

St. Paul Minnesota 26 October 1960

dear parents
he hails my mother and father
a biological label
a nod to what remains
of their primal power in his life.

a budget in words
he writes
the pastor will charge me $30 instead of $20 rent
business is business
and building a church merely flexing
and muscle.

send money

he's surprised that he's still
going with Linda after a month
she is a decent girl,
I hope I can behave.

he says so little
of any importance
small, measurable things, cooked in his mind
rise to the surface in this letter
leaving a watermark.

I cannot tell if the stains on this envelope
are the blur of his fountain pen
or the blue ink
of my mother's
tears.

SHAPES

St. Paul Park Minnesota
November 16, 5 pm 1960

I flex my right arm
to write to Thor.
I draw shapes.
a sun
amoeba
running people-shape
a fish with legs
a three-legged fish.

I've forgotten the story behind those shapes
but they were much simpler than Thor's mulling
about whether he should join
the debate team
to answer the burning question
should government control labour?

a good subject
but not as keen
as getting to the dentist.
this is imperative.

a fish with legs
distracts everyone from worry.

TRACKING

familiar etching of jackrabbit, coyote,
reading the creatures of small
discovering a rabbit warren
deep in an Alberta forest
the things my eyes have learned to see
after immigration.

I am seeking an address that is 40 years old.
the numbers on the envelope
no longer meaningless signifiers.
I can track them to our old house
to where Thor was nowhere
he was
not.

my bladder is full and strained.

my father told me
if you piss on a place, it is yours.
so like a bitch dog marking territory
I mark this place with my very own water.

if Thor should seek me here
he will find my scent
and wait.

ADDRESSES

Chinook clouds
merging with the bruise of the sky
make me dream
about a house that slides away from me
into no fixed address.

I thought I would find him there
my dead brother.
his cells realigned to now
in the signs of his choosing
his handwriting
håndskrift.

the address on the old envelope
simple, proto-postal code
found the right path after all
between Minnesota and
Calgary.

ONE NAME FOR SNOW

a life spanning ocean,
prairie roads, the St. Lawrence vein.
at eighty, my father eats an eight-ounce Alberta steak.

his eyes big
with privilege
surprised with blessing
and the colossal confirmation
that this steak is his to eat.

if my father remembers war
it is the Nazi occupation of Denmark
setting bombs on munitions huts
sniffing betrayal in a roundup of resisters.
he is still able to name
all the Danish words for soil:
jord, jordbund, smuds, snavs, svineri.

when he remembers the turning of his tongue
to English
he recalls bitter winters in Calgary
the evening news-hour listening
to the Old Indian at Morley
who divines the weather
as no European can.

my father learns to sound one English name for snow
avoiding a full expression of cold and white.
the prairie too large to speak its full name
my father learns to trust
the language, the knowing
sounded
by the Old Indian.

CHECKING FOR TROLLS

my father respects trolls.
he does not admit
to ever seeing one, but
trolls are not the sort of thing
you should talk about.

my father spent time looking for trolls
under arched bridges made in Denmark
millennia ago,
dark Latin stoneworkers merging
with Vikings
turning
into trolls.

the boy my father was is listening
for great hairy things
who exact a price for crossing safely
to the other side of the water.

my father does not admit
that he dreams of trolls
as he crosses the Atlantic
the roll and pitch of sky turning
to angry, grey water.

my father is silent
as he watches the errant wisp of a troll's beard
just at the periphery
of the St. Lawrence Seaway.

my father breathes deeply
as he crosses the prairie
spotting no bridges
where trolls might lurk.

when he hears the windy laughter
of barbed wire fences
on a flatflat prairie horizon
he chuckles, knowing
he has out-travelled the trolls.

FATHER LOVES JUNE

the season of prairie spring
when evening shadows move long
and peonies columbine with snap dragons, and smiles
in cheerful pansies.
poplar leaves forget their tremors
syrupy days
and nights hang heavy
like a lover's desire.

June promises my birthday
my mother's anniversary from exile
a pregnant Demeter.
my father blesses the blossom of June
a flower that bursts
returning his women to him.

I know my father's heartbeat like the pulse of trees.
in the strum of bees in June
his old voice throating contentment, thick pleasure
in his simple words *happy birsday*
he remembers the cost
of claiming
me.

THE JÆTTE

giants, or Jætte, dwelt in Jötenheim, or in Utgard, outside the limits of earth and sea assigned to them by the gods, just on the edge of Heaven. Fornjot, the old giant, was progenitor of the Jætte, father of Kari, the wind, of Hymir, the sea, and Logi, the fire.

The memories flick at me like snapshots, live, behind my eyes. The eyes that know the world as you have caused it to be. Trees and grass and flowers and names for things in Danish, rå and real.

My first snapshots of sleep on your wide chest, a landscape of comfort, hearing your heartbeat. Beat. With the slowness and surety of your belonging, in this country, and to me. I fall asleep to its sound, your arms cradling the small of me.

Heat. My body on fire and throwing up on the edge of my bed, alone, until your hands lie on my head, stroking, murmuring the dis ease away.

Roar of you in anger, rare, like thunder in December. Your long arms in a windup toward my bum. Frustration over something I did not hear the first time. Patience blown away like a loose shingle from a roof.

boulders, rocks, even islands were said to have been dropped by them as they carried them from one place to another.

English, the language you will not speak, saving the energy of words for the flow of your body, for the paint you put on everyone else's house, your arms grown longer in hard drag of the brush against wood and fiber.

Building a greenhouse against a neighbour's garage and planting beefsteak tomatoes and watching them grow into something like apples on a tomato vine. Asking 'what's your favourite colour, Daddy?' Pause. A look around you. 'Green'. Enough said. The word for vision of life inadequate for what we know as breathing inside each other. The wide curl of your pipe smoke caressing air like sweetgrass stroking sky.

You make a decision about me and my brother. Mom saying: 'I can't take those two fighting anymore, you have to help me keep them busy.' The next day we each have a paint brush, that extension of you, a dingy fence to paint, and orders to finish the job before you get home that night. I never knew that fence was so long.

the river Ifing, which never freezes, separates the realm of giants and gods.

Me wandering off to the trees when we first moved into our house on Immigrant Street, too little to know the perils, the fields full of mice, gophers, and places to explore. You out looking for me and me knowing I was in trouble. Your long arm stretching to me, winding me into your chest like a spool wrapping thread. Then pointing to the open manhole that was big enough to swallow me. A time before and after fear. A thing I did not know until you named it, caused it to be. You speaking the name of fear in English, which I learned then was the language of fear. You wanted me to know its name, smell its hide, and hear its sounds, so if separated from you, I could recognize the sewer I might fall into so easily. Away from the heartbeat in your warm chest.

Denmark had once been cultivated by Jætte; we know this from megalithic remains and boulders on hilltops.

The sound of values, of ethics, of burning, tortured, battered and bludgeoned bodies of Jews on the shores of Kollund in May of 1945. Wearing the armband of your Resistance to the Nazis. Waiting for invasion, guarding the borders of Denmark. Then, a body floating, you imagining invasion, then more and more, an endless school of dead Jews murdered the night before, bodies bayoneted and last screams shelling the dual shores of Denmark and Germany.

You were first to find them, gather them together like sardines, assemble them for burning. Finding the butcher who had a camera to record this Shiva. Telling me what he said that day: 'we take pictures of this because there will always be someone who will tell you that this never happened.' No use telling you that the war is over, because then no one will see these pictures and recall.

Vilhof, the Jætte of the Wood, lived in the wilds. When the soldiers of Eirik menaced, he led them astray by a delusive mist.

Searching the woods around Padborg, I half hope to find the remnants of your dugout, the one built into the lee of the evergreens like a den, stocked with food, clothing, warmth, your body becoming earth under these trees. The hiding place from the Nazis, ensuring that this place would not be searched if they saw a swastika flag on a stick embedded into your Viking mound.

At the end of Heaven, hence probably near Jötenheim, the Jætte Hræsvelg, 'Corpse-Eater', sits in eagle form, making the wind with his wings.

I dreamed about the knife last night, slid its thin blade carefully against my thumb, tested its cut. Smelling its metallic scent, knowing that its grey teeth would slice through a sandwich. For years, the best knife in our house, the one you retrieved from the pile of booty that the Germans left behind as they crossed the border after the war ended. Thin with age now, like you. Crossing the ocean, immigrating with us. A trophy of power you once had, a memento of history.

Thor was a great opponent of the Jætte, his hammer the great defense of the gods and yet Odin's descent was traced from the Jætte.

Lost now. You gave it to Thor, the only sword you had between you and him, your oldest son. The sword, passing it to him so he could die fighting, a great shout – into Valhalla. Lost now, its physicality. But I can still smell its forged metal in my dreams. The sword passed to me, your eldest daughter.

Jætte were often violent, especially when thwarted, their rage of 'jötenmodr', a frenzy of the Jætte.

The healing dream you had, a woman's voice calling: 'Thor, Thor', and you hearing this, like small Samuel the sound of his God. You getting up in this half-life of knowing, searching for your dead son, making your way to the front door and swinging it open to shout, 'His name is Thorkild, and it is written in the Book of Life.' No angel, no woman, no being, argues with you. Thorkild's knife-sword lost now, taken with him where the grave cannot go.

Jætte women were beautiful, beloved of gods and heroes.

And I am woman born of you. Breasts full and round and curves and wet bush. I am not woman without your manhood, and the heavy thump of your heartbeat. Beat. In the maze of my woman-ear.

HUNINN AND MUNINN

Thought and Memory: the two companion ravens of Odin

The Tree

HRÆFN

fate weavers
demanding
yet strangely content
with the dog kibble I toss them
to curry their favour.

when I hear them speak in the Old Norse tongue
naming themselves
Huninn and Muninn
Thought and Memory
I know they've been sent as wings
to my ceremony
my search for leylines.

battle birds, they return to Odin each night
telling what they have learned.

she is ready craaks Thought
we are well fed caws Memory

shape shifters
the trick, to let them hop beside me
as partners to my thoughts.

ravens keep my deepest secrets.

TWO SISTERS – B & W PHOTO

landings.

Moster says
the ground disappeared
beneath her feet.

she missed a sister for support
left to measure
the smallness of Denmark in the bones of her parents.

my mother picked stones
on a homestead in Alberta
made field notes
about starving Indians.
exposed lies
about hungry bears
long since culled from the prairies.

truths unknown in Denmark
but framed inside a steep prairie sky.

shadows and missings
blurry faces
positives and negatives
I find stored in boxes
originals sent to the Old Country

rediscovered in snapshots
reproduced
truths are actually
a merge of time
and old grief.

MOON MARES

i

when Moster talks, her words rankle like burrs
attach to my ears
like tics snatching at tender fur.

if I listen
I can hear Moster's haaawck
ready to spew.

she and Mother
are forever
black and white
negatives
two sisters, distant, binary,
corresponding.
two sides of the same moon.

I ask Moster to tell truths
then wait for her burrs of speech
Jeg foldt mange gang jeg stod helt alene I Verden
she felt all alone in the world
her life the narrowest of slivers in a cold
ancient Viking longhouse
like a fingernail clipping of a waxing moon.
she insists on the ebony comfort of a night sky
alone.

like the moon, aware that it waxes
Moster comes into her fullness
a savage orb rising
in the dog days of summer.

Merete loves the dry heat of Calgary
the honest, pacific, waves of Vancouver.
the craggy bruise of mountains against the sky.
the elemental curve
of horizon, a remaindering
of her mother's heart, and she writes:

men for din skyld lille mor, skal jeg nok komme hjem igen.
but for your sake, little mother, I shall come home again.

ii

Moster's burry voice in those letters
surprises my mother, who *had no idea my sister could write*
so eloquently about my immigration
or Merete's visit to Canada
or speak so well on important matters.

sister and sister have spent
too much time
gazing at reflections of the moon
in pond, river, lake, canal, ocean
where no voices could be heard.

neither able to ponder
the mares of depression in the moon
or collect them as cameos
of the face of the sun
they take for granted.

A BIG LIGHT

these two boys look for beacons
on a distant hill, a bright light to aim for
deciding who to follow
where to go.

this time, in this story
is their bond. the light
atop a haystack larger than both of them.

this tall place surveys all of Padborg, Denmark
these boys pack, like safe hounds
they imagine Skyld
what will be
from the scented foreshadowing
of a haystack.

these boys hold their lights high
aid each other's sight.
climb a haystack
to see the world.

the sweet sinless apprenticeship
of scaling this smallness
prepares them for beacons
and separates
          Knud-Erik, the one who will remain
          from Thorkild, the one who sails for Canada.

SØNDERSTROMFJORD

away from time
iced in glacier

Greenland in July is pockmarked inkpots
of flued ice and stone chipped
from the skin of a glacier.

before a life waiting to be written
I rested here, twenty-five years ago
midnight sun in the freshness I was then.

thousands of miles from millennia
I landed in Sønderstromfjord
a name longer than time
vowels locked like pools between rock

and bought a postcard I never sent.

returning now, riting
Sønderstromfjord
this ancient word that sings from my Viking lips
lace-frosted slip of Valkyrie
Greenland in April.
the name of long time approaching millennium
is now cream over chipped stone
on my tongue.

RINGING A BOAR

a memory that arrests me
    in a moment of pique; a flight of panic

Uncle Peter saying *watch now*
he clutches a steel ring, fingers taut and strong
around an iron circle.

we are in the pig barn, in the bowels of Denmark
where men and pigs and little girls
all smell the same.
the reek of boar assaults skin and clothes and hair.
each knows the other's power.

Uncle Peter leaps the fence
boar shriek pierces wall
rattles the pen.

I freeze the terror in this frame
where Uncle Peter leaps back out
barn dust settling in his shirt
Viking blue eyes gleaming at me.

hvor du bang, pige?
were you afraid, girl?

his human voice starts my heart. again.

if I leave this barn, I will fear nothing. again.
the freeze-frame recalled
in the classroom where the drunk threatens the women, I clutch
    my pocket knife.
where my husband pounds his fist in the wall, I stand ever so
    still.

where a man weighs on my body, his tongue swollen with booze
   that bites my breast,
I grip the ring.

if alive I leave this barn
I will know
how to ring a boar.

FACES ON PANSIES

sharp pansy pungence
mauve spice I breathe
in the same pulse beat as I know Tante Minna
follows me into her flowers.

she insists, cultivates
a lone prairie garden.

facets of colour highlight
petaled mickey mouse blossom ears
albino eyes
pollinated flower grins.

I feel a tug on the hem of my garment
prompting me to stop.
a half turn toward her,
the probe of her tucking.
she is placing
a pinch of laughing pansy faces
the last stitches of stories she sews
into the hem of my skirt
to bless me into places she will never go.

my dress is solid
with a hem full of smiling pansies.

ELVES AND WINTER SOLSTICE

It is an old Danish custom to leave rice pudding out on the winter solstice,
so that gifts are made to pacify the living creatures who might invade a
house in this dark time, and either help or hinder the occupants.

rats scurry in my attic
lured by the sweet scent of rice and rich cream
but they never trouble me.
it is a cheap offering
to rats and elves.

I checked my bowl today
the leftover rice was pocked with tiny foot wells.
the elves had been by.

I forgot to warn you to set out rice pudding for them
so they would distract brutality.

if I told you this trick
maybe the man who abuses you at Christmas
in a ritual all his own
would have found the rice and laughed
at elvish folly.

exchanged his fist
for rat's fur
a cat's supper.

COPENHAGEN SNUFF

afternoon delight
began in København
the summer I was nineteen.

long before AIDS
men coupled here, on the rocks of København
long since cobbled
between ancient stones in the streets.

my body tight
with youth
muscle
charged with flesh
conducting heat and storm

moving from København into the countryside of farmers
I fill my hands with the dirt of Denmark
touch the tongues of Vikings
the sky changes, graying the soils of me
English to Danish
root to ripening.

electric storms are wilder here.

COPENHAGEN POPPIES

scarlet, orange, golden petal-balloons attached
to lush green stalks that insist on staying, rooted.

balloons puffed with sea air
satisfied with their places
refusing flight.

I found them in July
i København
dust dry but so close to the sea
a misplaced meadow
here the poppies make no sense

like me, my bones and skin the brown
of Denmark, dry in July
and the soil of Canada suddenly foreign
here, in the bloom of blossom-balloons.
my fingers clasp around
green stalks, measuring the cut
and the colours, staining my hands.

I know this place: like the poppies that live here.

sauntering back to Uncle Erik's home
clutching poppy balloons
in the greening generation of Vikings.

ANNA DOROTHEA

as I dream the memories
not my own, of you
not my grandmother
snapshots form in sepia page
emerging from the peat bogs of Denmark.

you are a Tollund woman.

I have studied your wrinkles
and hollow eyes so well.

it is your story I know best
feel deepest in the marrow of vision.
the sepia tones of your flesh
grown cold, frosted
full of brandy
and the will to die
a Danish ditch as good as your bed.

1918 could only snap autumn gold sepia
and your cold death from Spanish influenza.
they said
I could not hold your soul
could not tell your truths because
my cells never incubated in the grotto of your cave
and for this you must forever be unknown to me.

if that were true, I could not write this poem
for the fever that killed you by brandy and slow burn
beckoned my Far Mor to your husband's bed.
a story spanning the length of this century
leaping over the boundaries of millennium.

I have named it the seepage of sepia
flowing into the lines of the palms of my hands
it touches my fingers.

and your death writes these lines
preserves
my flesh

for the truth of women is inside this stone.
unless you had died

I would never have become.

DIVINING, ONE

I love her splashing
her trust in water
enough to waste on sunblind, muddy, feet.
Tante Minna and Uncle Chris
move inland from Cochrane in 1934
eke a living
from the teats of Eric Harvie's cows.

life in the lowlands
where all they can eat or drink
leaks from a cow
or pads
softly
from willows.

Tante Minna sews underwear for six kids
from the neighbour's scrap pile of cloth.
the same neighbours that name her twins George and Elizabeth
to honour the King and Queen's Coronation.
Tante Minna shrugs. English names are best.
and besides, the right name solicits gifts.
the Harvies bring carriages, clothes for the babies.
the old farmhouse expands like a swollen river.
the whirl and thunk of a pump
divines, pulls water for a swelling home.

I tell Uncle Chris that he is clever for inventing such a thing.
he laughs, but I don't think I'm so funny.

Tante Minna in old age
is a grassy oxbow bank, her mossy old breasts
woo an underground river.
she wears gumboots
kicks them off to splash
in a spring-fed cattle trough
hears monody
of water, tumbling.

a doe emerges from a poplar birth
ambles along the leyline of this spring
twitches long ears
divining water, she stoops
drinks from trust
trickling from the earth.

DIVINING, TWO

*And behold, the veil of the temple was torn in two from top to bottom and
the earth shook; and the rocks were split.*

Matthew 27:51

i

A patchwork road to Cochrane, tufted with threads of bench
grass and brome; thistles cleave river rock, fossils gasping
through smooth stone and summer fallow fields. To the west,
an abandoned farm where you might kneel before the glory of
God and mountains. A tight turn into the old homestead.

Here lived two Scottish men, polo princes who thought to
purchase the privilege of water. The illusion of water lived here
in the Dirty Thirties, because the pump stands erect, steel
phallus alert with the old money of colonizers. Sitting on this
side of the 1A, I feel bereft of soul. The spring has dried,
leaving only my unease, the fervent desire to escape, like the
Scottish men. The old pump a tool of divination that falls short
of a biblical stick, and smashes against rock, revealing water.

ii

Across the 1A Highway

summer, fully sewn in finishing touches of
fescue, brome grass, silverberry, sage.
Tante Minna knows the fissure
where earth's seams are rent asunder.

she frees herself in ferns,
bleeds, in her moontime, over wet moss
nibbles on wild oats
sticks her toes in
the lode of secrets
a rare aquifer where water, licketing stones
shifts shape.

she knows how to drink
from leaks in the ground that open like desire.
variegations of thirst, whetted, she dares to fantasize
slivers of intention.
lifts her voice to a kyrie of wet cascade
alone, splashing in water as clear as a laugh
old feet
nurtured by secret springs.

THE MEANING OF ORANGE

the petals fall in the fountain
the orange-coloured rose leaves
their ochre clings to the stone
Ts'ai Chi'h
Ezra Pound

in a rare rainstorm on the prairie
the land of drought glows, shocked
at the smashing flay of water.

orange is the colour of surprise
lane borders on the highway
broken or solid.
the word that has no partner
for how would you couple
with surprise or shock?
or accept a pelting of rain
on barley, parched.

orange is a shock of millennial hair on a teenager
a bleached stain of nonconformity
a modern version of an ochre paint job
creating a useful mask.

the orange full moon is startled by a thief
disguised as the sun
a flashlight trained
on a night orb
reminding the moon of who's in charge.

orange is the silky skirt of a wood lily
or the meaning I give to the inside of a sunset
or the vision of my Danish grandfathers
and the peculiar promises they wrought from pigs.

marigolds, flashing
warning the worms.

in a rare touch of ochre,
tumbling mustard, sowthistle, goatsbeard in passion
embarrassed by the exposure of light
sunflower, locoweed yellow, forced to orange.

the tease of a river, old in oxbow
stroking the breast of moss on a southbank.

two oranges, their weight like breasts
claiming the fullness of open palms
allowing no other grasp.

when the rapture occurs
I will taste orange light
bite into salvation's juice
and shed the ochre challenge
of a mask.

TOWARD SKYLD

I carry
an artifact of the future
where a search
for the vulva shells of Norns
takes an unexpected turn.

Tante Minna's voice is Wyrd
as she says to me *take it, just take it.*
she means the old picture
the one of her mother, Anna Dorothea, and all five siblings
the one that none of her children want
or so she believes.

in the same way she believes
she can bake sepia memory
into a fold of me that will leaven in time
and open
when I need real food and sustenance
from a crone, a wyrd woman.

I feel her thrusting me
in a crone's spin of blindman's buff
toward an unknown direction.

I am baked into a future
where no one would think to look.
I am passed invisibly beyond borders she could not see
become the Skyld of her voice
saying *take it, just take it.*

CLOUDBURST

hazy light in June
when sun struggles through memory's floss
heaving a scent of rain.

this light steals me into being
five years old, home, safe from kindergarten.
a long walk away with my tall brother
who scoops me up, like cool sand.

I become
as tall as he.
he is Thor, muffled thunder
and warning of rain
who whispers *you must go to school.*
as he utters this phrase
a sharp raindrop baptizes
my forehead.

he promises
to walk me home
if I wait at the school for him.
he promises
to give me Koolaid outside
in my favourite Yogi Bear glass.

hand in his, I remind him of his promises.
but just before he pours the juice
I toss the glass into the air, casting joy like rain
then lose it.
in wet June light
shards burst on the sidewalk.

joy was just emerging
from the alchemy of risk
turning light to rain to glass
shattered. I see Thor
alive yet, wet, shocked by breaking sound
in a glass half empty,
half full, of moments, the memories
just before cloudburst.

SPRING MIGRATION

years after the long walk
the one I took with you
down the hospital hall, holding your arm
seeking
the wall bars and steering your hand
toward them.

years after the long walk
I pick up the scent of caribou.
Thor-thundering rumble of thousands

migration as relentless
as hell-red sun
and velvet itchy antlers softened
into your brow.

years before the long walk
in the season of your waiting, Yoho spring
your awe
waiting for the caribou
to pass
giving you time to rest before you continued the journey.
not a damn thing you could do about it anyway.

years after the long walk
you shed velvet into bloodied bone fingers
and readied for a fight.
the tumour above your right eye
shattered into blood.

DOPPLER EFFECT

(for Eric)

Doppler: a memory of movement;
in physics, the apparent shift in the frequency of sound, light, and other
waves caused by relative movement between the source and the observer.

your lean youth, unfettered with memory
approaches me
augured in light
in the place where
your grandfather leaps

from a convertible in 1960
dances the twist with a smaller me, his little sister.
white t-shirt sleeves wrapped
around a package of cigarettes,
at eighteen, the frequency of his face
coming atcha now, taken for granted like
the fast, bad joke physics of genes
imbedded in the grooves of your flesh.

but you can't see him
for *he* becomes *you*
in the moving memory that waves at me from 1960
my dead brother, Thor
dancing, the twist
your grandfather,
leaping from your car, alive!
I cry
into August heat
                    waves.

ACKNOWLEDGEMENTS: I wish to express my gratitude to the Alberta Foundation for the Arts for a Junior Writer's Grant to begin this project, and to the Eastend Arts Council for my stay at the Wallace Stegner House to complete the collection.

My thanks to Bob Stallworthy for revealing so many ways of reading between the leylines. To all the Jordmorer: Sharon Butala, Bryson LaBoissiére, Kathy-Lynn Treybig, my aunts, mothers and cousins who told me the stories. A special thanks to Eva Tihanyi and Helen Bajorek MacDonald, who heard the heartbeat and helped me breathe through the pains. To Glenn Burgess, who supported me and listened patiently through it all as well as helping me to write with my broken arm: my love and kudos.

A very special thanks to Cecelia and John Frey and to Catherine Fuller, all of whom knew how to honour the runestenen of women's words.

Some of these poems or variations thereof have appeared in *Descant, A Room of One's Own*, and *SLANT Magazine*. Material quoted in the poem *Impedimenta* is reproduced courtesy of the Canadian Plains Research Center, University of Regina, from Craig W. Miller (ed.) *Union of Opposites: Letters from Rit Svane Wengel.* Material cited in *The Jætte* is from *Mythology of All Races: Eddic Mythology, vol. 2,* MacCulloch, J.A., Canon John Arnot and George Footmore (Consulting Editor) Cooper Square Publishers, Inc., New York, NY, 1964. Chapter XXVII, "Giants", p. 276-284.